To

From

Flavia®

Because You're My Friend
copyright © 1993 by Flavia Weedn
All rights reserved. Printed in Singapore.

For information write Andrews and McMeel,
a Universal Press Syndicate Company,
4900 Main Street, Kansas City, Missouri 64112

ISBN: 0-8362-4700-0

BECAUSE YOU'RE
MY FRIEND

Written and Illustrated
by Flavia Weedn

Because

you're

my

friend

we've

shared

dreams

and tears...

FLAVIA

laughter

and

disappointments.

You know
the things
I dream of

and

the things

I'll never

be.

You're

always

there

when

I need

you

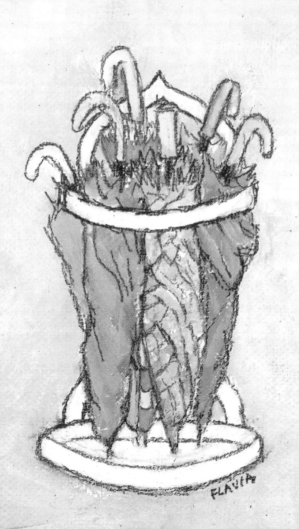

and you

listen and

you understand.

I'll

always

be here

for you

and I'll catch
you if you
should fall.

I'll care
how you
feel when
you lose

and be

with you

when you're

afraid.

You'll

always be

a part of

my life...

because

you're

my

friend.

Flavia at work in her Santa Barbara studio

Flavia Weedn is a writer, painter and philosopher. Her life's work is about hope for the human spirit. "I want to reach people of all ages who have never been told, 'wait a minute, look around you. It's wonderful to be alive and every one of us matters. We can make a difference if we keep trying and never give up.'" It is Flavia's and her family's wish to awaken this spirit in each and every one of us. Flavia's messages are translated into many foreign languages on giftware, books and paper goods around the world.

To find out more about Flavia write to:
Weedn Studios, Ltd.
740 State Street, 3rd Floor
Santa Barbara, CA 93101 USA
or call: 805-564-6909